HOW MUCH DO YOU KNOW ABOUT ANIMALS?

WELCOME TO

HOW MUCH DO YOU KNOW ABOUT

ANIMALS?

Can you get all the questions right?

ENJOY!

Which animal is the odd one out?

The DOG is the odd one out!

Which animal makes the sound "QUACK"?

The DUCK makes the sound "QUACK"!

Which one of these cannot fly?

The SNAIL cannot fly!

Which animal likes to eat bananas?

The MONKEY likes to eat bananas!

Which animal lives in water?

The **DOLPHIN** lives in water!

Which animal is the odd one out?

The SEAHORSE is the odd one out!

Which animal lives in the desert?

The **CAMEL** lives
in the desert!

Which animal makes the sound "ROAR"?

The LION makes the sound "ROAR"!

Which animal likes to eat hay?

The HORSE likes to eat hay!

Which is the odd one out?

The **FISH** is the odd one out!

Which animal likes to eat nuts?

The SQUIRREL
likes to eat nuts!

Which animal lives in a dark cave?

The BAT lives in a dark cave!

Which animal is the odd one out?

The KANGAROO

is the odd one out!

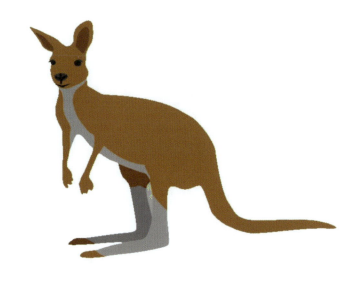

Which animal makes the noise "OINK?"

The PIG makes the noise "OINK"!

Which animal likes to eat carrots?

The **RABBIT** likes to eat carrots!

Which animal cannot walk?

The SHARK

cannot walk!

THE END!

Printed in Great Britain
by Amazon